To Paul

With

and the

welcomes to Surrey

Ricks, Rao,

Russy + Oils

xx xx

THE VILLAGES OF
Surrey

ANDY WILLIAMS & GRAHAM COLLYER

COUNTRYSIDE BOOKS

Counties in our colour portrait series include:

BUCKINGHAMSHIRE	LEICESTERSHIRE
CHESHIRE	LINCOLNSHIRE
DEVON	SUFFOLK
DERBYSHIRE	SURREY
DORSET	SUSSEX
ESSEX	WARWICKSHIRE
HAMPSHIRE	

Other counties in this series include:
DORSET
HERTFORDSHIRE

First published 1995
Photographs © Andy Williams 1995
Text © Graham Collyer 1995
Reprinted 1999

COUNTRYSIDE BOOKS
3 CATHERINE ROAD
NEWBURY, BERKSHIRE

ISBN 1 85306 362 2

Designed by Mon Mohan
Produced through MRM Associates Ltd., Reading
Typeset by Paragon Typesetters, Queensferry, Clwyd
Printed in Singapore

Contents

INTRODUCTION

Surrey is a county of contrasts. Urban development and rural landscape. Busy motorways and country lanes. One million people suggests overcrowding, but Surrey is not densely populated. There are large and medium sized towns but no cities. There are many villages and hamlets and they are what this book is about.

This is a celebration, in colour, of the county's glorious villages. They may be very different from those described by John Evelyn, John Aubrey and William Cobbett, but the names are the same. Gone is the dependence on agriculture. A thing of the past, too, are the cottage industries. Villages in today's Surrey do, of course, have farms and pockets of local employment, but increasingly they are inhabited by people who have moved in, buying up property, and who travel into the towns or up to London to conduct their business. These are the new villagers and they have changed the face of our rural areas. But if it were not for them many of the communities would have withered and died.

Evelyn, Aubrey and Cobbett, were they to return, simply would not be able to comprehend what they saw before them. Cobbett, of the three, was the last to die, in 1835. But just consider that this was 10 years before the railway came to Guildford and that the beginning of the motor car age was still at least 60 years away.

A more recent authority on Surrey was the late Eric Parker, of Feathercombe, Hambledon. He was largely of this century and his writing style and eye for detail have left us with an unsurpassed record of what the county was like from the later years of Queen Victoria's reign through to and beyond the Second World War. Parker knew every corner intimately and he wrote with clarity and precision.

Surrey is my county. I was born in Rowledge, near Farnham, close to where Cobbett had his roots. He and Eric Parker have influenced my view of the area more than any other writers. I make no apologies for repeating some of their comments in this volume. Together, I believe, they are able to convey the real Surrey.

And the real Surrey, for me, is the villages. Of course, Guildford is a fine county town and its High Street and historic Guildhall are without parallel, but so many of the villages are quintessentially English and, in spite of the relentless pace of change and the onslaught of traffic, they have stood the test of time and are still beautiful.

Photographer Andy Williams knows a pretty village when he sees one, and he has produced some wonderful scenes for this book. He has been able to prove that Surrey continues to be a county of enchanting landscapes. Much of it is in the hands of the National Trust, still more is protected by the County Council and 11 local authorities – but it is for every one of us to cherish the countryside. It is our heritage.

And in Surrey it is a particularly rich heritage.

Graham Collyer
Hindhead, 1999

Frensham

Most people will know Frensham Great Pond, but not necessarily the village. The Great Pond (*inset*), and its smaller neighbour on the other side of the King's Ridge, are great favourites with sailors, anglers, walkers and riders. They were made in the 13th century to supply fish for the bishops of Winchester, who resided in Farnham Castle. The ponds are situated on Frensham Common, much of which is owned by the National Trust and managed by Waverley Borough Council. There is a real sense of open space when you stand on top of the King's Ridge, and the views can be breathtaking.

Frensham village nestles to the north of the Great Pond and St Mary's church is tucked away down a lane that leads to the old mill and on to the hamlet of Dockenfield before the border with Hampshire is reached. At the church is the curiosity known as Mother Ludlam's Cauldron, a large vessel which, legend states, came from a cave in which the White Witch of Waverley lived. The diarist Aubrey dismissed this theory as nonsense and suggested the cauldron had been used for village feast days and weddings. Whatever its former function, it is a popular local artefact and the story of Mother Ludlam lives on in the folklore of south-west Surrey.

Frensham parish, much smaller now than in the 1920s when it included Hindhead, as well as Shottermill on the southern side of the A3, continues to contain Churt where the former prime minister David Lloyd George had his country home for more than two decades before his death in the early 1940s. He farmed a large area on the slopes of Hindhead, successfully turning what had been inhospitable land into productive fields and orchards. Lloyd George's influence can still be seen today and he is depicted on the sign of the Pride of the Valley inn, which stands close to where he had his house.

Tilford

There is a timelessness about the scene at Tilford when cricket is played on the village green. Even the traffic seems not to intrude while the sound of leather on willow resounds across the perfectly formed triangle. For more than 110 years Tilford Cricket Club has played its matches here and because of its picturesque setting the green attracts visitors in large numbers. There is always plenty going on, and it is surrounded by fascination. The two narrow bridges are believed to have been built by the monks at Waverley Abbey, little more than a six hit away. The Institute beside the green was designed by the renowned Surrey architect Sir Edwin Lutyens. The river Wey's two branches join here, behind the Barley Mow whose beer has slaked thirsts for nigh on 200 years.

Perhaps the most fascinating of all is the venerable oak which, observed Cobbett in *Rural Rides* in 1822, was the finest tree he had ever seen. Alas, the ravages of time have wreaked their havoc on this noble specimen, whose age is nothing like the 1,000 years so many writers would have us believe, but more like 350. It gave its name to the house that stands beside it, a place that, in cricket circles at least, is famous and known throughout the world. For this was the home for the last 40 years of his life of William 'Silver Billy' Beldham, the greatest player of his age, who retired to Oak Cottage after a long career through the late Georgian and Regency periods. Beldham was a colossus on the cricket fields of England, including the three in London made by Thomas Lord, and died in Oak Cottage in 1862 at the age of 96. Whether or not Beldham observed Cobbett measuring the old tree in 1822 is not known, but he would have looked out on that rural scene with a keen eye for four decades. He was never idle and kept a string of visiting writers entertained with tales of his cricketing exploits. The centrepiece of his living room was his bat which, 120 years after its owner's death, was tracked down by this writer and is now back in south-west Surrey, where it was made in 1815.

Hindhead and Grayswood

Hindhead Common, which includes Gibbet Hill and the Devil's Punch Bowl (*opposite*), was among the first tracts of open space acquired by the National Trust, one of whose three founding members was Sir Robert Hunter, who lived close by at Haslemere. Public subscription bought the land after its owner, the financier Whitaker Wright, had committed suicide following his conviction for fraud in the early years of the 20th century. The death of Wright, who lived at Witley Park, had the developers licking their lips at the thought of getting their hands on his land. Fortunately, a quick and spirited campaign raised the necessary money to purchase the common, which, in turn, was given to the Trust.

Gibbet Hill is so named because of a celebrated murder there of an unknown man in 1786. It is the second highest point in the county and dominates south-west Surrey. Beneath it, the Devil's Punch Bowl is a breathtaking scoop of wild land, whose many moods are dictated by the weather. The only blight here is the constant stream of traffic on the A3, which runs between hill and bowl.

The growth of modern Hindhead was begun in the 1880s when Professor John Tyndall built a house on the summit. He was an engineer who visited Switzerland every year for the good of his health, but when he discovered the solitude and clean, fresh air of the pine-clad hills of Hindhead he knew that at last he had found a place in England which, too, could be beneficial. His coming prompted other prominent men and women to settle in the area. Tyndall's home still stands but no longer 'four square to the winds of heaven'. It is on the edge of the common, from where there are good walks to Haslemere and to Grayswood, the latter via Gibbet Hill and its neighbour Hurt Hill.

Grayswood's green and church (*inset*) are pretty, but all too often missed by passing motorists. As this is splendid walking country it is good news that the Wheatsheaf public house has been saved from closure after a strong lobby by local residents.

Chiddingfold

The annual bonfire night celebrations in Chiddingfold go back 150 or so years and now attract around 10,000 people. They are as big as any in the county and money raised is given to the elderly of the parish at Christmas. The anniversary of Guy Fawkes' attempt to blow up Parliament shows no sign of ending in the village, but it might not have progressed beyond 1929 had certain people had their way.

In that year, 250 police officers were dispatched to the village when the scene turned ugly as word got out that a local bobby had been responsible for firing the bonfire in advance of the day. The Deputy Chief Constable led police from all over the county to ensure order was restored after local residents had rained stones and fireworks onto a sergeant and a justice of the peace.

Such was the alarm that another JP stood by to read the Riot Act. Pubs, which do a roaring trade on bonfire night, were ordered not to open, but in the event the evening passed peacefully, the Riot Act went unread, and Chiddingfold folk regarded the whole affair with amusement. Police over-reaction might be considered a suitable headline today.

Chiddingfold is the largest of the Fold villages and its prettiness is a tribute to those who strive so hard to keep it clean in spite of the constant stream of traffic on the main road that cuts right through its heart. It was a great glass-making centre and examples of the work of local manufacturers are to be found in St Stephen's Chapel at Westminster and St George's Chapel at Windsor. There were eleven glass works on the village green in the reign of Elizabeth I. Now, of course, there is none.

Brook and Witley

The Dog and Pheasant pub and the cricket ground on the opposite side of the road are great attractions for visitors to the small village of Brook (*opposite*) in the parish of Witley. If you approach from the north, you will notice that one side of the road is bounded by a high wall that clearly was impressive when it was built at the turn of the century. At that time it was described as 'the finest in England' and enclosed the Witley Park estate of the financier Whitaker Wright. He paid £37,000 to have the six miles of wall built, but that was small change when compared with the £840,000 his mansion set him back and the further £500,000 he spent on landscaping the park, including a lake under which there was a glass-roofed ballroom. Wright's extravagances came to an abrupt end when he was convicted of fraud in 1904 and, while waiting to be taken to prison, swallowed a cyanide capsule. William Cobbett knew Witley Park as Lea Park and often stayed there.

Witley Common, now owned by the National Trust, was home to billeted soldiers during both World Wars and is some distance from the village which gives it its name. The A3 borders it before climbing southwards towards Hindhead.

There was a church in Witley (*inset*) mentioned in the Domesday Book, and All Saints is one of the seven churches in the county containing Saxon work. It was always one of Surrey's ecclesiastical treasures, but assumed even greater importance when wall paintings from the 12th century were found. A three-tiered fresco representing scenes from the life of Christ was uncovered in 1889, having been limewashed over during the Reformation, but it was to be more than a century later that another great work of art, depicting the *Harrowing of Hell*, came to light.

Witley has a station on the Waterloo to Portsmouth line, and this makes the area attractive to people who commute daily to London. But this movement alters the pattern and pace of village life. Nevertheless, it remains as one of a number of south-west Surrey villages where there is a feeling of community, as well as picturesque buildings for the visitor to enjoy.

Peper Harow

Now that an A3 bypass has been built, the thunder and roar of traffic in Milford has been considerably reduced. To the west of the new road is Peper Harow Park and mansion, once the home of the Lords Midleton, the fifth of whom engaged the architect Augustus Pugin to build Oxenford Grange on the park's southern boundary. Pugin's brief in 1844 was to produce a farm and gatehouse in the likeness of the grange that had stood there until 1775. Oxenford was farmed by monks from Waverley, the Cistercian abbey founded on the banks of the river Wey near Farnham in 1128 and whose dissolution in 1536 led to much of its masonry being used in buildings elsewhere in the district. The grange that Pugin copied was 13th century and might well have been built by the monks, whose other work included bridges across the Wey, notably at Tilford, Elstead, Eashing and Peper Harow.

The mansion at Peper Harow was partially destroyed by fire a few years ago, but has been restored. It is a fine building which can occasionally be glimpsed across the park and a view at close quarters is recommended. The present house was built in 1775, close to the original home of the Brodricks (subsequently the Lords Midleton) which had been erected in the early part of the 18th century. Great Cedars of Lebanon trees which dominate the park were planted as seedlings from pots in 1735, and the ground on which the Peper Harow Cricket Club plays was laid out around 1720 by Alan Brodrick, the son and heir of the first Lord Midleton. It was the scene of great matches whose rules were very much the foundation of the present Laws of Cricket.

Peper Harow Park and the commonland around Milford are criss-crossed by a network of footpaths. It is gentle walking country and there is a variety of scenery, flora and fauna to be seen in the area immediately to the west of the A3.

Puttenham and Seale

The charm of Puttenham (*opposite*) has been retained in spite of the ravages brought on by modern living. Two major roads form an eastern and a northern boundary to a parish which endeavours to sit quietly beneath the Hog's Back, the chalk spine of the North Downs between Farnham and Guildford. Puttenham remains essentially a rural community. The majority of its hop fields may have disappeared but there is still a small pocket of a once great industry to be seen. Some of the farmland may be set aside but tractors working in the fields close to the village centre continue to be a common sight. Puttenham, which is so close to the heart of Guildford, illustrates how well town and country sit side by side and how successfully green belt policy has protected from development even countryside that is barely more than a couple of miles from the centre of the county town.

The National Trust owns Puttenham Common, beloved of walkers and riders, below which are the six stretches of water collectively known as Cutt Mill Ponds. The Tarn is the largest and popular with anglers. It is separated from Cutt Mill Pond by a causeway which takes the road from Puttenham to Elstead. Between The Tarn and the great house at Hampton are Warren, General's, Long and Trout Ponds.

Puttenham's church of St John the Evangelist is in a dominant position at the head of the main street through the village, and there can be few artists and photographers locally who have not sought to include its features in their collections. From Puttenham to Seale is a pleasant, twisting journey through soft countryside sheltered by the Hog's Back. The church of St Lawrence at Seale (*inset*) sits in a hollow below the North Downs and work by the Waverley monks can be seen here. But Seale, which was never more than a hamlet, is just a shadow of its former self after the closure of the school, the post office and the shop.

Eashing and Shackleford

Although only a stone's throw from Britain's busiest trunk road, there is a timelessness about Eashing (*opposite*). It is no more than a collection of houses and cottages, a pub and a new business park adjoining the site of an old mill, either side of a much older crossing of the river Wey. The bridge with its seven arches was built by the monks at Waverley and is owned by the National Trust, along with adjacent roadside dwellings, bought for £400 in 1902. Because of its situation in a valley, Eashing has long been favoured as a river crossing and so the monks' 13th-century bridge provided a dry footing for the weary travellers on their way across the south-east of England.

With the realignment of the A3 at Eashing – the old Godalming bypass opened in the 1930s – made necessary by the construction of the Milford bypass, came a footbridge at the entrance to Eashing, or Lower Eashing as local residents prefer it to be known. This bridge takes the walker and rider onto farmland and the parkland of Peper Harow, from where Shackleford can be reached.

Shackleford (*inset*) is a spread out parish with many attractive houses and some fine architecture. The church of St Mary, which stands on the crossroads well away from the village centre, was designed in 1865 by Sir George Gilbert Scott, the prominent architect whose work also included the Albert Memorial in London. Aldro School in the centre of the village was built as a mansion in the last century on the site of Hall Place, which William de Shackleford owned in the reign of Henry VIII and which was demolished in 1797.

Littleton and Compton

It is probably true to say that more people discover the hamlet of Littleton every year; not because there is anything new about the place that prompts a visit, but because drivers in their desperation to avoid traffic jams will try every available alternative route. And the lane through Littleton (*opposite*) just happens to provide a short-cut to and from Guildford when the going gets tough on the A3 and the A3100. It is tough, too, on the handful of people who live there. The lane is barely wide enough for two vehicles to pass and consequently verges are systematically destroyed. When the motorists have gone and order has returned, then Littleton is a gem. The tiny church of St Francis, where there was also once a school, and its adjacent house sit in perfect symmetry.

Littleton was part of the Loseley estate and the great Elizabethan house is close by. Loseley was built in the 1560s by Sir William More, on the site of an earlier house, and he used material from the dissolved abbey at Waverley. It has been in the same family for more than 400 years and really is a delight to visit. As at Peper Harow, there are footpaths across the park and from here walkers are able to get onto the Pilgrims' Way and the North Downs Way between Guildford and Compton.

Compton (*inset*) attracts visitors for a variety of reasons. The Withies and the Harrow have been popular inns for many decades, and the church of St Nicholas possesses, says the Surrey Archaeological Society, the unique feature of a double sanctuary and also the oldest piece of Norman woodwork known in England. The Watts Gallery and the Watts Memorial Chapel, both in Down Lane, are constant reminders of the fact that the Victorian painter George Frederic Watts lived at nearby Limnerslease. Watts is buried at the chapel, which his widow, using Compton pottery as well as labour, built in the shape of a Greek cross.

Shalford

The village is so close to the centre of bustling Guildford and yet it has the appearance of being separated by a much greater distance. This is because development to the south of the county town has been halted almost before the High Street is out of sight. It was a bad day for conservation when, in the second half of the 1960s, the planners allowed the riverside development of what is now Debenhams store. It is a monstrosity beside the old town mill. However, once it and the pleasing shape of the Yvonne Arnaud Theatre are behind you there really is very little to cause displeasure. Mostly, the wedge between town and village is taken up by Shalford Meadows, the flood plain which has certainly done its job since 1968 when Guildford suffered its last spectacular flooding.

Shalford, like most villages, fares badly at the hands of the internal combustion engine. But away from the traffic there is rural peace. The Wey Navigation and its towpath provide good boating and walking between Godalming and the Thames at Weybridge, and Shalford, with its three public houses close to the river, is popular with ramblers. Those who wish to be more energetic can strike out from the village green and its cricket ground and climb Chinthurst Hill to obtain good views across the area.

Unless you are on foot you will probably not see Shalford Mill, which is tucked away off the main road. It came into the ownership of the National Trust in 1932, having once been in the Godwin-Austen family, whose good deeds are recalled on tablets in the early Victorian church of St Mary, across the road from the mill and near a cluster of little cottages.

Bramley

If you are a cricket historian or a railway buff you should know of Bramley. The village these days is troubled by traffic which gnaws away at its very fabric. It is a problem that has concerned local councillors and highways experts down the years with little result, save some so-called traffic calming measures, to show for all their huffing and puffing. A Bramley bypass is the stuff of dreams. There is, though, a thriving community spirit and two campaigns in recent years underline the point. The first saw a veritable army of residents and outsiders marshalled against the Surrey Probation Service, which sought to site a bail hostel in the village. Victory was the result. The second saved the village school from being closed as Surrey County Council's education department implemented changes to the ages at which children moved from primary and middle schools.

It was a different story in the 1960s, when the axe wielded on behalf of the Government by Dr Beeching fell on Bramley, with the result that the village lost its railway line and its station. The line from Guildford to Brighton via Horsham had served this part of Surrey for 100 years and its passing is mourned to this day. In fact, there is a body of opinion that believes the link should be re-established, but this is probably just a pipe-dream. However, when you stand in the centre of Bramley and risk life and limb as huge trucks thunder through you cannot help but ask yourself whether the policy that gave Dr Beeching his authority was somewhat misguided.

During the Second World War, a German fighter plane opened fire on a train as it passed through Bramley, killing a number of passengers. That was a sad occasion, but it took enemy action of a Whitehall kind to bring the line to its knees for good.

Gosden Common, on the way into the village from Guildford, was where the Maids of Bramley played their counterparts from Hambledon, near Godalming, at cricket in 1745, the first recorded match played by women.

Wonersh and Shamley Green

Old cottages and the Pepper Pot in the centre of Wonersh (*opposite*) make an attractive scene. Both are susceptible to heavy traffic, and the Pepper Pot has got in the way of long vehicles on a few occasions and required restoration. The villages between Guildford and Cranleigh are in many ways similar but each has distinct characteristics. Wonersh, with pretty cottages and gardens, was once dominated by the Grantley family of Wonersh Park. The first Baron Grantley, formerly Sir Fletcher Norton, was Speaker of the House of Commons from 1769 to 1782. It was his grandson, George, who, perhaps, left more of a mark, not so much for great deeds but for misdeeds. When he kidnapped his own children and held them at Wonersh Park, his wife, Caroline, quite naturally fought tooth and nail to get them back. This family affair became a cause célèbre and in 1839 led to the Custody of Infants Bill being enacted. Grandfather was by then long dead, but 70 years after he first sat in the Speaker's chair, Parliament brought in legislation directly as a result of his errant grandson.

The old house and the high wall that the Grantleys built to prevent prying eyes from looking in have long gone, although Wonersh Park remains as an estate of comfortable homes, and the Grantley Arms public house in the centre of the village ensures that the family name remains.

The neighbouring village of Shamley Green (*inset*) is in the same parish but has its own identity, centred around the green, and its Romano-British history. Oliver Cromwell knew it as Shamble Lea and granted a charter for an annual fair.

Hascombe and Busbridge

The White Horse at Hascombe is a good place from which to start and finish a walk. There are so many paths which radiate from the pleasant pub, some with a gradient that gets the heart thumping but leaves you wanting to quench your thirst. Try the one immediately behind the inn and you will soon be on a climb to the top of Hascombe Hill. At 644 ft it is high enough to give a decent view back across the village in the valley below. Iron Age Britons had a camp of nearly six acres on the summit, but when it was excavated in 1931 few remains of any note were discovered. Pottery from 150 BC gave some idea of when the camp was used, probably as a refuge from marauders in the settlements scattered about but now long since disappeared.

Today's Hascombe is a quiet backwater surrounded by rolling countryside, much of it wooded. The celebrated Winkworth Arboretum (*inset*) is close by, and so, too, is Hydon's Ball with its clear views to the north and the south. Both beauty spots are owned by the National Trust, and on Hydon's Ball there is a stone seat to the memory of Octavia Hill, one of the organisation's three founders.

Winkworth Arboretum was the idea of Dr Wilfrid Fox, a consultant dermatologist who lived nearby. Although knowing little about gardening, he turned 60 acres of scrubby hillside into beautiful groves and glades and gave the land to the Trust in 1952. Before he died in 1962, the Trust had bought a further 35 acres. Dr Fox is buried in Busbridge churchyard, close to the grave of one of the most famous of English gardeners, Gertrude Jekyll, much of whose life was spent in the area south of Godalming.

Busbridge Lakes (*opposite*) wildfowl centre has been established in the grounds of Busbridge Hall, a late 18th-century house, demolished in 1906 and replaced.

Dunsfold

It is hard to find a village in south-west Surrey that is more off the beaten track than Dunsfold. It is not really on a road to anywhere. There is a feeling that time has stood still here more than in any other village in the county. And yet why should this be when for more than 50 years there has been a strategically important airfield in the vicinity? Dunsfold Aerodrome, once a wartime base and now the home of British Aerospace's Harrier jets, is the major employer south of Guildford, but apart from when the planes are overhead there is little evidence of it being a neighbour. Even the Hawk and Harrier pub in the village had a change of name before going out of business altogether.

Dunsfold's houses are ribboned along the road through the village, but set back from it by a wide expanse of grass. Those who look for the parish church will not find it here. St Mary and All Saints is some distance from the main group of homes, down a lane past typical south-west Surrey cottages and really quite isolated. It is 13th century with a 15th-century wooden belfry, and well worth a visit. Notice, too, the venerable yew close to the porch. At 1,000 years, it looks its age, but it must be preserved at all costs. Surrey has some marvellous examples of yew and Dunsfold's is one of the best.

There is an air of timelessness about the church, and when you sit in those ancient pews you know that countless thousands of worshippers and visitors, for over 700 years, have done as you are doing. There is, perhaps, no place in Surrey for making you feel so humble. When you leave the churchyard by the lychgate, turn right and visit the Holy Well where the water, which is said to be like that at Lourdes, is reputed to heal disorders of the eyes.

Cranleigh

Cranleigh is claimed to be the largest village in the country although, it must be said, other places make a similar boast. It is the size of a small town, but the residents dismiss the notion that it should become one. There are all the modern conveniences, but it was not always thus. Cranleigh was as remote as any Wealden village until the trains came in 1865. They brought a prosperity that has lasted to this day and outlived the railway.

The great estates of Baynards and Knowle are on the outskirts of the village. Baynards, rebuilt after a fire in recent times, was originally built by Sir George More of Loseley, near Guildford, in the 16th century. Eric Parker has a story of the ghosts of Baynards and Loseley. It was said that after Sir Thomas More was executed, his daughter, Margaret Roper, brought his head to Baynards, which was her home. Thereafter, the ghosts of the two houses dined with each other, first at Baynards and the next year at Loseley.

Near to Baynards is Vachery Pond, built in the Napoleonic Wars as a source of water for the Wey and Arun Canal, a long lost but not forgotten waterway which linked the Surrey river at Shalford with the Sussex Arun, and provided a navigable route from the Thames to the English Channel at Littlehampton. Its heyday was before the coming of the railway; today, conservationists strive to recreate what they can of it.

In the medical field, Cranleigh was a pioneer back in 1859 when it opened the first cottage hospital in England. The Village Hospital was founded by Albert Napper, a surgeon in the village, who had the support of the rector, Archdeacon John Sapte. The necessity for such an establishment might have been prompted by an emergency when Mr Napper had to amputate a man's leg on the kichen table of a cottage. As a result, the rector, who served the parish for 60 years, offered Mr Napper a cottage free of rent and soon there were six beds and an operating room available for use.

Pirbright

This is a somewhat cut-off part of Guildford borough and borders both Woking and Surrey Heath districts. It has a large expanse of green in the centre and huge areas of common, much of it owned by the Ministry of Defence, around the edges. Pirbright regularly features in the Best Kept Village competition awards, so dedicated is its parish council to keeping the village spick and span. It can be no easy task, particularly in view of the volume of traffic using the roads through the centre.

On the green stands Lord Pirbright's Hall. It was built at his lordship's expense in 1899, two years after Queen Victoria's diamond jubilee had been celebrated with a fête on the green, given by Lord and Lady Pirbright who, as a commemoration of the occasion, donated a drinking fountain to the village. The couple lived at Henley Park and were generous benefactors. In 1901, to mark the accession to the throne of Edward VII, they provided the community with the land for a recreation ground.

The squat tower of St Michael's church was built with stones dug from the local commons. Just inside the churchyard is a much larger piece of granite which marks the grave (*inset*) of Henry Morton Stanley, the Welsh-born American journalist who came to live in Pirbright. He had, however, wanted to be buried in Westminster Abbey, next to Dr Livingstone, the Scottish explorer with whom he will for ever be associated. 'Dr Livingstone, I presume' has become part of our vocabulary, having first been uttered by Stanley in 1871 on the shores of Lake Tanganyika. Stanley, then 30, had been sent to Africa in search of Livingstone, and in true journalistic style he got his scoop and made his name.

Brookwood Cemetery, opened in 1854 by Act of Parliament, is close to Pirbright and the scene of the last resting place for thousands of civilians and service personnel. Its upkeep and future arouses stong feelings and passion, and attracts worldwide interest.

Wood Street and Worplesdon

The widespread parish of Worplesdon, immediately to the north of Guildford is split into four villages – Fairlands, Jacobs Well, Wood Street (*opposite*) and Worplesdon (*inset*) itself. All have their own identity. Much of the parish is the wedge between the boroughs of Guildford and Woking and is a mixture of residential development and open space. Fairlands, for example, is a housing estate but it has a village feel and a community of its own. It is separated from Wood Street by fields and commonland. Both have the word 'Village' attached to their name, and certainly the latter with its green and cottage gardens argues its case well.

Jacobs Well first appeared on the Worplesdon tithe map in 1839 but no one seems to know why. There are wells but who was Jacob? It must have been a very different place in those days. The London to Portsmouth road would have meandered close by before veering to plunge down Guildford High Street, and the road to what there was of pre-railway Woking would have been a dusty track. Jacobs Well would have been considered distant from both places. Now, though, Guildford's northerly spread is within its view.

The railway came to Worplesdon some 150 years ago, but the station, which is an important commuter link on the Waterloo line, is some way from the village centre. In the age before the railway, Worplesdon also had a station on the semaphore line from the Admiralty to Plymouth. That link, which was never completed, branched off the London to Portsmouth signalling line at Chatley Heath and messages were received and passed on at a tower next to the parish church. This early 19th-century form of an information superhighway lasted for six years until the line was abandoned in 1831, and the Worplesdon Glebe station was demolished 20 years later.

Chobham and Windlesham

Cannon Cottage (*inset*) stands beside a busy junction in bustling, attractive Chobham. The village has a prosperous and well-heeled look to it and people visit from miles around for its shops and restaurants. It is sufficiently distant from the main towns to be able to have a commercial identity without losing its uniqueness.

The tightly-knit centre is dominated by the 800-year-old St Lawrence church, in which can be found a chest which is almost as old and a rare eight-sided oak panelled font. There is also the tomb of Nicholas Heath who, having been sent to the Tower of London, was released and allowed to retire to Chobham. He had been Bishop of Worcester under Henry VIII but fell foul of Edward VI. He was restored by Mary Tudor and rose to be Archbishop of York and then Lord Chancellor, in which position he proclaimed the accession of Elizabeth I in the House of Lords. Heath bought Chobham Park from Queen Mary for £3,000 and he was visited there by Queen Elizabeth before he died in 1578.

Almost 300 years later Queen Victoria was in Chobham but for an entirely different reason. On 21 June, 1853, she came to review more than 8,000 troops who were camped on Chobham Common. It was styled a 'grand military picnic' and the monarch's visit is recalled by a memorial stone erected soon after her death.

Chobham Common was ideal for troop manoeuvres but in spite of the military continuing to take an interest in the area, it was at Aldershot, not so many miles away, that the 'Home of the British Army' was established later in the Victorian era.

The residential appeal of Chobham is in part due to the M3 motorway, which gives access – one hesitates to say easy access – to London. Beyond the motorway is Windlesham (*opposite*), where the church of St John the Baptist was erected in 1680, four years after a lightning strike had badly damaged the previous building.

Englefield Green and Virginia Water

It is the area to the north of this large village on the Surrey-Berkshire border that draws thousands of visitors to it every year. Runnymede and the Magna Carta Memorial, together with two other memorials on Cooper's Hill, are huge attractions. The Magna Carta is part of our history and our heritage and, put simply, has come to mean freedom and liberty. King John and his team of advisers travelled daily from nearby Windsor to negotiate in the meadows beside the river Thames at Runnymede, and the Magna Carta was finally issued over his seal on 15 June 1215.

The memorial to this event was the second of the three to be built on Cooper's Hill, which was given to the National Trust by Egham Council after Runnymede had been donated to the Trust in 1931. Its design was by Sir Edward Maufe, one of whose other great works in Surrey is Guildford Cathedral. The memorial was commissioned by the American Bar Association in 1957 and paid for by the contributions of 9,000 of its members. Four years earlier Maufe had designed the Air Forces Memorial (*inset*) on which the names of 20,456 airmen with no known graves are recorded. They lost their lives in the Second World War, either over the British Isles or the lands and seas of Northern and Western Europe.

The assassinated American president John F. Kennedy is remembered in the third memorial, erected in 1965 and unveiled by the Queen. It stands on an acre of land given to the United States by Britain, and the Portland stone plinth with three steps records that President Kennedy died 'by an assassin's hand' on 22 November 1963.

The three memorials bring together dates that are indelibly recorded in the memories of people everywhere. Almost 750 years of world history brought together in one small corner of Surrey.

At nearby Virginia Water (*opposite*) there are attractive woodland walks beside a 120-acre lake, which was created by the Duke of Cumberland after he had defeated Bonnie Prince Charlie at Culloden in 1746.

Pyrford

Beside the river between Pyrford and Ripley stand the lonely ruins of Newark Priory. Like Waverley Abbey near Farnham, it was once a great religious house but now its remains are but a reminder of another age. Newark was founded by Ruald de Calva and his wife, Beatrice de Sandes, for the Augustinian order in the reign of Richard I (Coeur-de-Lion) towards the end of the 12th century. There probably was a building on the site before the priory.

This is where the Wey splits into several streams, with the main channel being part of the Wey and Godalming Navigations, a 19½-mile waterway, owned by the National Trust, to the Thames at Weybridge. The Wey Navigation, from Guildford Town Wharf to the Thames, opened in 1653, almost 100 years before most other canals. It was a bold experiment, designed to change the natural river into a fast route between Guildford and the London docks. The attempt succeeded. Working barges have travelled up and down the Wey Navigation for over 300 years. The waterway brought prosperity to Guildford and new work to many local people. In 1763 the river was made navigable to Godalming, so forming the Wey and Godalming Navigations. Harry Stevens, the last private owner of the Wey Navigation, gave it to the National Trust in 1964. The Trust was subsequently given the Godalming Navigation by its trustees in 1968.

Now, where there were once barges full of cargo, there are pleasure craft. Boathouses at Godalming and Guildford hire out fully equipped narrow boats, and the navigations offer an interesting journey through gentle countryside.

Eric Parker wrote that a 'May morning on the Wey Canal rings with singing. You can count scores of cuckoo gliding in the sun and calling from the budding branches; woodpeckers laugh from oak to oak; plovers tumble in the wind; herons flap up lazily at a bend in the stream, and flap lazily down again; snipe cut high arcs in the blue and drum down from the sailing clouds; perhaps from the very heart of the thicket the nightingale bursts into a pulsing riot of song.'

Times may have changed but the navigations, considering that they are so close to urbanisation, can still be a place of beauty, surprise and solitude.

Ripley

Ripley was a mecca for cyclists long before the motorist took over. It was far enough down the old Portsmouth Road for Londoners to be able to ride out, have tea and then return home. And dispensing the teas were the sisters Dibble, who became so popular in their lifetime that when they died cyclists clubbed together and paid for a stained glass window in their memory to be placed in the parish church.

Annie and Harriet Dibble were kindly, church-going souls who ran the Anchor Inn. It was 25 miles from the centre of London, and the sisters knew exactly how to cater for ravenous cyclists after a long, bumpy and dusty ride from the capital. For a quarter of a century up to 7,000 cyclists would visit the Anchor every year. Their machines were nothing like the sleek models of today – they were boneshakers and penny-farthings. The riders who flocked to the door of the Dibble sisters, and who even had the Bible read to them, were for ever in their debt, and it was a very sad day when Annie died in July 1895 and Harriet 15 months later.

As the car replaced the bicycle so the Portsmouth Road became more busy. Ripley, because of its village centre attractions, became impassable and the clamour for a bypass reached a crescendo, with the result that the A3 was realigned to the east and much of the through traffic was removed. If the Dibbles could return they would not find the Ripley they knew – but it is more pleasant than it was, 25 or so years ago.

Long before the Dibble sisters were drawing huge numbers of visitors to Ripley, the national spotlight was on the village because of its cricketing exploits. Ripley green is one of the oldest cricket grounds in the country, and for around 250 years the game has been played on it. Surrey County Cricket Club had its origins on pitches like this one, and the great players of the late 18th and early 19th century appeared here in matches, such as 22 Surrey men v England in 1802.

The Clandons

Two great houses, both owned by the National Trust, mean that the twin villages of West and East Clandon are known far beyond the county boundary. Clandon House (*opposite*) stands in its own park on the Guildford side of West Clandon. It was first built in the Elizabethan period, and the present Palladian mansion dates from around 1730. Clandon was the work of the Venetian architect Giacomo Leoni for the second Lord Onslow. The park was laid out by the great landscape gardener, Lancelot 'Capability' Brown. Sir Richard Onslow was Speaker of the House of Commons in 1708 and was enobled eight years later. His grandfather, also Sir Richard, had been the Speaker under Elizabeth I and had purchased Clandon in 1642. Today the house, with its enormous entrance hall, attracts visitors from all over the world, and in particular from New Zealand where a later Lord Onslow had connections and was responsible for bringing to Clandon a wonderful Maori pa (meeting house) which had escaped the devastation caused by an earthquake near Rotorua around 100 years ago.

At Hatchlands in East Clandon (*inset*) there is an important collection of early musical instruments, put together by the tenant, Alec Cobbe. Admiral Edward Boscawen, an 18th century naval hero, started the house in 1756, and two years later Robert Adam, on his return from the Grand Tour, was given his first commission in England. The library, drawing room and staircase hall were all the work of Adam, but towards the end of the century the staircase was altered by Guiseppe Bonomi, who put a large window on the half-landing.

Both houses are well worth a visit, but so, too, are the villages. West Clandon's St Peter and St Paul's is on the site of a Domesday church which, said John Aubrey, fell down 'a small time before Christmas in 1716' and was rebuilt by 'the contributions of parishioners'. The ancient church of St Thomas of Canterbury stands among a delightful collection of houses and other buildings in the smaller village of East Clandon.

Wisley

The Royal Horticultural Society gardens at Wisley are known throughout the world, and they attract visitors from all parts of the globe. They are a haven of peace and tranquillity, just a short distance from the A3 racetrack and the M25 bottlenecks. When the RHS moved from Kew to Wisley in 1904 all was very different, of course. The London to Portsmouth road was full of cyclists, especially at weekends, and the motor car and the charabanc were only just beginning to be more regular modes of transport.

The early gardens were a third of their present size. The society's treasurer, Mr G.F. Wilson, owned 60 acres of shrubs and flowers at Wisley, and when he died they were purchased by Sir Thomas Hanbury and given to the RHS. Whether Mr Wilson would have approved of the growth and the changes at the gardens cannot be known. Eric Parker, who knew Wisley in Mr Wilson's day, said later, 'Experiment and officialdom have settled heavily on its sandy soil, and the wilder charm of the old pleasance has left it.'

The church at Wisley has no dedication, and is beyond the gardens on the lane that leads past one of Surrey's many new golf courses and on to the Wey Navigation at Pyrford. Back beside the A3 there is a small lake known as Bolder Mere, but long gone is the Hut Hotel which stood on the opposite side of the road. It was demolished to make room for the widening of the busy trunk road. All in the name of progress.

Cobham

Like Cranleigh, Cobham is really a small town, so much growth has there been in recent times. It was always an important stop on the old Portsmouth Road, and on Chatley Heath to the south, in an earlier age, the semaphore tower was an integral part of the link from the Admiralty to Portsmouth and the junction for the unfinished line to Plymouth via Worplesdon and the Hog's Back.

Now that the A3 races away on a bypass, Cobham has regained some of its sanity. Down beside the river Mole it is at its best and here the National Trust has Cedar House (*opposite, right*), a Georgian-fronted building with some parts behind as old as 15th century. It stands close to the site of Cobham Mill, which was recorded in the Domesday Book.

The beauty of Painshill Park has been restored in recent years. The park was the creation of Charles Hamilton, youngest son of the sixth Earl of Abercorn. The area was bare heath when Hamilton came by it in the first half of the 18th century. Having burnt the heather and broken up the land by growing turnips, he set to work on establishing the gardens that became a source of wonderment and attracted prominent people as visitors. Two who came were Presidents Jefferson and Adams of the United States, so too did Horace Walpole and John Wesley.

Another great name associated with Cobham is the poet Matthew Arnold, who lived for his last 15 years, until his death in 1888, at Painshill Cottage. A local road is named after this famous literary figure.

Stoke D'Abernon

Not only is the church of St Mary the Virgin at Stoke D'Abernon the oldest in the county but it has the oldest brass in the country. The church at Stoche, as it was known in the Domesday Book, was built around AD 650 but little from that period remains. The D'Abernon family are recalled by the brasses of father and son. Sir John senior, who died in 1277, is depicted as a knight armed with a lance. The brass memorial to this one-time Sheriff of Surrey is the oldest in England. Close by is a memorial to his son, also Sir John, who died 50 years later. Together, these brasses make the church at Stoke D'Abernon an important stop on the ecclesiastical historian's trail.

Such was the influence of the D'Abernon family that they gave their name to the village. They were, said Eric Parker, a 'knightly family' but they did not provide an English king with a great soldier, or a great politician, 'or with anything much more than the quiet services of a country gentleman'.

All this was 700 years ago. The village has seen so much change but the church, which is one of just five beside the Mole and the only one on the banks of the river, and the brasses remain as visible reminders of the depth and richness of our history and heritage here in Surrey.

The Horsleys

West and East Horsley, like the Clandons nearer to Guildford, are twin villages with much to commend them. The photograph opposite shows the curious gatehouse that guards the entrance to Horsley Towers at East Horsley. Travellers on the road to Leatherhead from Guildford cannot miss it, but what they do not catch a glimpse of is the Towers, a mid-1800s extravagance by the Earl of Lovelace, who was responsible for so much of the rebuilding in the eastern village.

Lovelace left his mark with some distinctive buildings, much of them in local flint, but the Towers did not suit Eric Parker who, in noting that there were some superb beeches in the park there, considered the 'grey coldness' of Horsley Towers was 'a little exotic among these stretches of southern English parkland'.

He continued, 'Good Jacobean or Georgian red-brick much better suits oaks and beeches than the chateau-like towers of a Scottish castle.'

The two churches, St Martin in East Horsley and St Mary the Virgin in West Horsley, are very old and full of interest, but undoubtedly the story that captures the imagination more than any other here is the one about Sir Walter Raleigh's head being buried in a vault in the south chapel of St Mary's. Raleigh's widow kept the head in a red leather bag for 25 years and then his younger son, Carew, who had inherited West Horsley Place in 1643, placed the skull in the vault. More than 50 years later the head was apparently seen when the wife of the new owner of West Horsley Place, who had lost her life during the Great Storm of 26 November 1703, was also laid to rest in the tomb.

Chilworth

The photograph on the opposite page could have been taken in any number of locations in Surrey. It is a typical farm gate opening up to a gorgeous downland view. This gate, in fact, is close to Chilworth, a linear village on the North Downs Link railway line, from which access to the ridge is easy and picturesque.

High above Chilworth is the small chapel of St Martha (*inset*), a wonderful spot to stop and explore and to admire the views. From St Martha's you can see for miles, and you can also set out on the Downslink path that will take you to the South Downs.

The dedication of the chapel has always puzzled people. A strong possibility is that it is a corruption of Martyr, going back to the Normans. Tradition has it that Christians were martyred there by pagan Saxons around AD 600. The earliest documentary evidence of the name Martha appears about 1200, and Bishop Waynflete of Winchester wrote in 1463 of 'the chapel dedicated to Saint Martha the Virgin and all the Holy Martyrs, commonly called Martirhill founded and situated next to the town of Guldeforde in our diocese'. By the mid-1800s the chapel was a ruin and as forlorn as the abandoned St Catherine's on its hill beside the old Portsmouth Road out of Guildford. Then, the Surrey architect Henry Woodyer undertook restoration work and it once more became a place of worship.

Down in the village in former times there was a flourishing gunpowder manufacturing industry, and thanks to Surrey's industrial historians there is an informative walk through the ruins. Chilworth Gunpowder Company was not formed until 1885 but explosives were made there as early as 1580. There were several serious incidents; one, in 1763, rocking the neighbourhood and bringing the tower of St Martha's crashing down. Then, in February 1901, there was the last great disaster which claimed the lives of six workers. The works closed for good in 1920.

Shere and Albury

Most who write on Surrey are agreed that Shere (*opposite*) is the prettiest village in the county. Eric Parker needs to be quoted here. In 1908, he wrote, 'If Shere is to be counted the prettiest Surrey village of all, I think it is the Tillingbourne which decides the choice. The village groups itself with the little brook running through the middle. A low bridge crosses the stream, villagers sit on the bridge, white ducks paddle about the current and stand upside down among the weeds. Beyond the brook are the tiny village green and the shade of elms. On one side of the village green is the old inn, the White Horse; and on the other the grey tower and the quiet of the churchyard. But it is the sparkle and the chatter of the Tillingbourne which are the first charm of all.'

So many writers have attempted to follow Parker's lead and to encapsulate the glory of Shere. But he was the master among Surrey authors.

Attractiveness has a price in the modern world and Shere pays heavily, the village centre being simply overrun by vehicles and visitors. Whether pedestrianisation and a one-way traffic system can be the solution remains to be seen. One thing is certain, it will not stop people from visiting the village. But if they have to leave their vehicles away from the centre then that will not be a bad thing. Shere can never be returned to the place that Eric Parker knew in 1908, but it surely can again become more tranquil.

At neighbouring Albury, the great chimneys (*inset*) by Augustus Pugin are eye-catching. He built them in the middle of the last century at the same time as he was engaged in the rebuilding of the Houses of Parliament after the major fire there in 1834. At the Shere end of Albury is the disused Catholic Apostolic church, built in 1840 at a cost of £16,000 for Edward Irving, who came south from Scotland and started the Irvingite Sect which so captivated Henry Drummond, banker and politician, who owned Albury Park and was finally responsible for the old village moving from the park and being established on its present site.

A Romano-British temple on Farley Heath, nearby, dates back to AD 100. Martin Tupper excavated it in the last century and found more than 1,000 coins and other objects.

Abinger Hammer

If Shere is the prettiest village, then Abinger Hammer, its close neighbour to the east, has the best known landmark. Overhanging the A25 for almost a century, the clock is as much photographed as that fine timepiece

in Guildford High Street. 'By me you know how fast to go' is its legend, and the blacksmith figure strikes the time on the hour.

The clock was given in memory of the first Lord Farrer of Abinger Hall, who died in 1899. It is a potent reminder of just how important was the iron industry in the area, the Tillingbourne stream being dammed in several places to create the heads of water required by the iron masters in their ancient craft. Now the ponds have been converted for use as watercress beds, the clear water of the chalk stream being ideal for this salad crop, which is one of a range of products – trout from the Tillingbourne being another – being promoted by the Taste of the South East group. The produce of Surrey, including the fine wines from the Denbies estate at Dorking, the largest vineyard in England and little more than 10 years old, and the smaller estate at Godstone, have for too long been underestimated, and while other counties have sought to market their individual home-produced ranges of foodstuffs, Surrey has remained largely silent. Now this has come to an end, and the taste of Surrey is being widely advertised and accepted for what it is – excellent value.

The Farrer seat at Abinger Hall has been demolished, but it was where Charles Darwin made his observations about the earthworm. Up on the North Downs behind the old hall is a memorial stone marking the spot where, in 1873, Bishop Samuel Wilberforce of Winchester was fatally injured when his horse tripped and threw him.

Coldharbour and Westcott

Rising above Coldharbour, which, at 750 ft, is the highest village centre in the county, is Leith Hill, whose summit is 967 ft above sea level and, by 72 ft, the highest spot in Surrey. The tower (*opposite*) on top of Leith Hill was built around 1765 by Richard Hull of Leith Hill Place, who, when he died seven years later, was buried underneath his folly and, apparently, upside down – so that he might one day face his Maker the right way up. Perhaps he knew Major Peter Labelliere, the eccentric Marines officer from Dorking, who, in 1800, was buried on Box Hill, overlooking Leith Hill, the wrong way up so that 'when the world was turned topsy-turvy he might come right at last'.

Leith Hill is owned by the National Trust and it and Coldharbour are popular places for walkers and ramblers. Iron Age Britons had a large camp at Anstiebury, a hill close to the village, and, while the modern visitor is hard-pressed to make out its form, it was considered worthy of being used again when Napoleon was threatening our shores in the early 19th century. Word went out to the good people of Dorking that they would need to take refuge at Anstiebury if Napoleon got a foothold here. In the event, they did not have to leave their homes, and Anstiebury was left to its memories.

Coldharbour, like so many of our villages, is a victim of the motor car. Its narrow lanes were not designed for them, and the best way to see it and the surrounding countryside is by leaving the car well out of the way.

Westcott, to the north, is on the A25 and in spite of, or perhaps because of, the M25 its buildings resound to the noise of passing traffic. Sir George Gilbert Scott designed the church that stands on a bank above the road. On the green there is a dovecote with a weathervane whose symbol for north is not 'N' but 'T' – arrange the letters to spell WEST, add COTT, and what do you get?

Great Bookham

The great house, Polesden Lacey, and 1,000 acres of estate were left to the National Trust in 1942 and besides being one of its foremost properties in the south it is also the headquarters of the Trust's Southern Region. Polesden Lacey's donor was the hostess Mrs Ronald Greville, who, over nearly four decades, entertained royalty and most of society's leading names. Edward VII was a close friend, so too were King George VI and Queen Elizabeth who spent part of their honeymoon at the house.

Like so many of our major houses and churches, Polesden Lacey stands on the site of an earlier building. This one was commenced in 1823-24 and replaced the home of the dramatist and politician Richard Sheridan.

He had bought the property in 1797, along with 300 acres, and had lived there with his second wife until his death in the early 1820s. Polesden Lacey's splendid grass terrace was begun in 1761 and extended by Sheridan, and the Doric columns at one end of it once formed the portico of the house.

Down in the village of Great Bookham the church of St Nicholas is Norman on a Saxon site. The wooden tower is unusual in that it stands on what is thought to be a Norman stone base. Two windows uncovered in 1913 are believed to date back to the time of the Domesday Book. The rector for half a century until his death in 1820 was Jane Austen's godfather, the Rev Samuel Cooke.

Brockham and Betchworth

Thousands of visitors pour into Brockham (*opposite*) to celebrate Guy Fawkes Night. The annual bonfire rivals that at Chiddingfold as the largest in the county. If you can get close enough, the blaze and the fireworks display are well worth watching, but get there early and be prepared to walk the last mile or so.

On that dark night in November the majority of the spectators will enter and leave the village without ever knowing anything of its true identity. Brockham is delightful. With a backdrop of the North Downs, scarred in places by quarrying, the cottages and houses look a picture in the spring and the summer. The whole area is well cherished, and over the years the judges in the county's Best Kept Village competition have awarded it several prizes.

The river Mole, on its journey of 42 miles from Sussex to the Thames at Hampton Court, meanders gently through the countryside. But it has another side after heavy and prolonged rain, and often bursts its banks hereabouts.

Christ Church, on one side of the green, is a memorial to Henry Goulburn, who was Chancellor of the Exchequer in Wellington's government and Home Secretary under Peel, and whose key offices of state were held during the reign of four monarchs. Kenneth (now Lord) Baker, the former MP for Mole Valley, held several high offices, including that of Home Secretary, in Margaret Thatcher's governments, and as a resident of these parts must have felt an affinity with Goulburn.

Those who do not leave the A25 do not get to know the charms of both Brockham and Betchworth. The latter has a station on the pretty North Downs line, but the village is to the south of both railway and main road. Perhaps not so well known as Brockham, it is without doubt an attractive place, with an old church (*inset*) and pub, and a golf course.

Leigh

If you ask the way to 'Lee' you are just as likely to be sent to Lancashire or to any of the many places whose names are pronounced in that fashion. This is 'Lye' and the reason has been lost in the mists of time. The village is one of the smallest in Surrey and sits prettily around a green with a weatherboarded pub, the Plough, and the church of St Bartholomew in close proximity. Today, Leigh is little more than a dormitory village, and in that respect no different to so many others. It is still some distance off the main road but nowhere near as remote as in Elizabethan times, when it was exempt from the Act of Parliament that prevented timber over a certain size from being burnt to fuel the iron industry. The reason, it is thought, is because of Leigh's position, which would have prevented heavy and long trunks being transported over the poor local roads.

There are some fine brasses in the 15th-century church, including those to the Arderne family of Leigh Place, one of whose subsequent owners was Sir Thomas Copley, a distant cousin of Elizabeth I. A lady in white is said to haunt Leigh Place.

Modern Leigh probably cares little about the Ardernes and the Copleys, and the other great medieval families who resided around here. However, it will identify with Ben Jonson, who used it as a retreat from busy Elizabethan London. Jonson, friend of Shakespeare, were he to return today, might not agree that Leigh is still worth retreating to, what with aircraft using nearby Gatwick and the modern home's need for at least one car, and probably three, because of the absence of a practical public transport system. Living in villages such as Leigh is all very well and good, provided you have the means to get about. And that puts pressure on narrow, country roads and lanes, still no wider than when Jonson was around. Perhaps he might think that the so-called hustle and bustle of the London he knew and frequented was not so bad after all.

Chaldon

The *Ladder of Salvation* is thought to be the work of a monk 800 years ago and it has been bringing visitors to Chaldon for more than a century. It is a huge wall painting, more than 17 ft by 11 ft, and after years of being hidden by a covering of whitewash it was rediscovered in 1870 by workmen who were restoring the 11th-century church of St Peter (*inset*). The work, which occupies most of the west wall of the church, is said to be 'archaeologically at least . . . the most valuable and interesting wall painting in England.'

Chaldon is a small village up on the North Downs near Caterham. It was once as remote as any village in the county, but motorway travel and the growing tentacles of Croydon and Purley have brought suburbia ever closer. However, for all the change around it, Chaldon remains a community, with its famous wall painting in St Peter's one of the treasures of Surrey.

The photograph opposite is not of Chaldon but of a rural scene close to the Sussex border in the south-west of the county. However, at harvest time it is representative of much of Surrey, which, in spite of its one million people and the many miles of motorway, said to be more than in any other county, continues to be a place where there is a rich pattern of rural life, a wide variety of breathtaking scenery and a broad patchwork of landscapes. Long may that remain to be the case.

Godstone and Bletchingley

William Cobbett had a soft spot for Godstone (*opposite*), and it is easy to see why. Even today, with a traffic-dominated village centre, there is an appeal about the place, although what Cobbett would make of the noise and the fumes one shudders to think. His rides often took him through the village and he would stop at the White Hart to eat his countryman's lunch of bread and cheese and bacon. He liked what he saw in 1822. 'The gardens are all very neat,' he wrote, 'and, at the inn, there is a nice garden well stocked with beautiful flowers in the season.' Cobbett described Godstone as 'a beautiful village, chiefly of one street with a fine large green before it and with a pond in the green.' The green and the pond are still there and are very much still the jewels in the crown. Cobbett would like that. But if only the traffic volumes on the A25 and A22 would decrease (has the M25 to the north made any appreciable difference?), Godstone would again be the calm, peaceful village that the great writer, politician, and man of Surrey, waxed lyrical about all those years ago.

Bletchingley (*inset*) lies to the west of Godstone on the A25 and was one of Cobbett's 'vile rotten boroughs' with its two Members of Parliament.

Nowadays, it is picturesque and much photographed, especially the 14th-century Whyte Harte Inn close to the church of St Mary, whose origins are Norman. There was a castle which was one of the first to be built in the county, but it was destroyed in 1264, little more than 100 years after it had been constructed.

Lingfield and Crowhurst

It is well over 100 years since the village cage in Lingfield (*opposite*) was used as a lock-up. In its heyday it had a chequered existence, with many a drunk, rogue or vagabond being thrown into its darkened interior and spending a cold night there to await release, probably with a headache and a hangover,

or to be taken on a visit to the nearest magistrate.

Today's Lingfield is very different and is well known nationally as a horse-racing centre. Lingfield Park racecourse has had an all-weather track for some years, in addition to the more usual turf, and offers racing throughout the year.

The church of St Peter and St Paul is often referred to as the Westminster Abbey of Surrey and is set amid fine old timbered buildings. There are many memorials associated with the Cobham family, who lived nearby and were a force in the land in medieval times.

North of Lingfield is the small village of Crowhurst, where the fascination of seeing a yew tree (*inset*) as ancient as any in the country draws countless numbers of visitors to the churchyard every year. The church of St George is 800 years old, but the tree is much older. How much, no one knows, but it could be 700 years. Local tree specialists believe it could survive for another 500 years, by which time it might be 2,000 years old. The yew is well protected, and survived the great storms of 1987 and 1990. Indeed, younger neighbours were blown down, including one 95-year-old which had provided shelter for the old 'un.

Visitors will notice that the tree has been hollowed out and a door attached. This was done in 1805, and a table and seating for twelve men were arranged around the interior. It was in all probability a drinking den and on Palm Sundays long ago when a fair was held around the yew it was said the 'ale flows free and mirth rises high'.

Titsey and Limpsfield

The motorway to the north has taken much traffic away from Limpsfield but the village is not entirely free from the menace of the car culture. The A25 continues to be a busy road and is often preferred as an alternative and, some would argue, less stressful and on occasions quicker route between Surrey and Kent. The county boundary is just beyond Limpsfield and the National Trust owns 350 acres of open space as Surrey ends.

The composer Frederick Delius is buried in Limpsfield churchyard (*inset*), in spite of the fact that he was born in Yorkshire of German origin and died in France, where he lived for much of his life. Delius, born in 1862, encountered parental opposition when he wished to pursue a musical career, but in time he met Grieg and was encouraged to be his own man. He settled in France and his compositions became popular on the Continent. Sir Thomas Beecham introduced his work to this country and, by the time he died, Delius had become one of our best known composers. Beecham led a torchlight funeral oration when the body of Delius was reburied at Limpsfield.

Above the motorway and underneath the North Downs is Titsey, and the photograph opposite shows the church of St James, which was built to replace the original church when, in 1776, the owner of Titsey Place, Sir John Gresham, did not wish to have the building only 35 ft from his front door. So he knocked it down and St James's was erected outside the estate boundary. There is not a lot else at Titsey, but it is a good area for walking with the Downs so close.

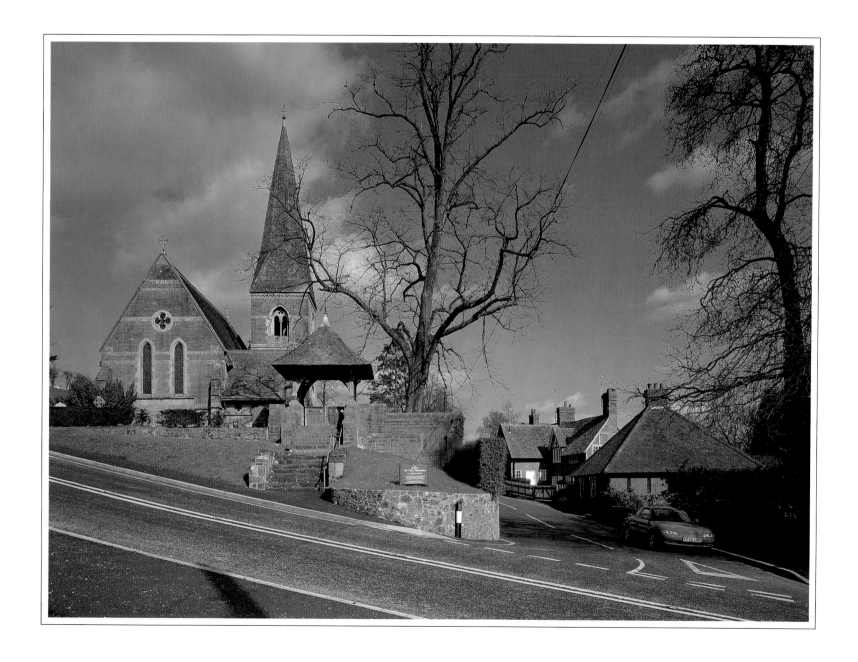